Psalms & Stones

Poems by Wm. Anthony Connolly

Spartan Press

Kansas City Missouri

Spartan Press
Kansas City, MO
spartanpresskc@gmail.com

First Edition 1 3 5 7 9 10 8 6 4 2
ISBN: 978-1-950380-19-0
LCCN: 2019937763

Design, edits and layout: Jason Ryberg
Cover image: Jon Lee Grafton
Title page image: Wm. Anthony Connolly
Author photo: Dyan Connolly

Acknowledgments:

Some of the poems in this collection in slightly different versions have been published in literary journals or been broadcast. "The Pole of Relative Inaccessibility" was produced and aired on CBC Radio's *Alberta Anthology*; "Levaya," was published in *Timeslice: Houston Poets 2005* published by Mutabilis Press; "Slow Lone Burn," appeared in the inaugural edition of *The Esthetic Apostle.* "Altoids and Cigarettes" "Ice Story" and "Sweetness" were published by Colorado State's Nieve Roja. "Guf" was part of the Columbia Art League's Interpretations exihibit and book publication.

CONTENTS

Psalms

Stones

Psalms & Stones

For Dyan

Inspired by Jane K, Franz W. & Kevin R.

Psalms

Words & Weeds

There are no words
Sometimes too many for what's at hand
Out to the unruly backyard, an embarrassing
Array of thorn, thicket, weed cover, dirt
What nature has done needs attention
Cutting the grass its sweet pungent reward
Over mud-furrows and stubborn ground ivy
Picking up after the trees their limbs astray, akimbo
To marvel at the rabbit pathways, the light
Through the veil of this tiny forest
To sweat, swear, and finally breathe
Earning an iced tea, a few moments to gather
Yourself a dull pencil sharpened, you begin
Again

Daybreak Prayers

We take our waking slow
saying our daybreak prayers
there is no hurrying escape
the warm heart of morning
this belief in close holding
bodies wrapped in love,
denying the day its due.

Happy You Are Home

Fed cat sunning on the deck.

Palm fronds dripping with sunlit water,
Dry grass sucking up gulps of drenched loam—
Inching deeper.

The evening sky scrubbed, rinsed
Retiring—
Dog, stuffed toy clamped in its panting grin—
Happy you are home.

You say traffic was bad
Can't believe we do it every day—
But we do.

We do—
To be here for this
The inching deeper.

Guf

On the night you died
My broken father in heaven
Plainchant upon your chest
God is almighty
Rising
Falling
Hallowed be your name
Falling
Give us
Falling in the end down
This day
Our daily
To the shoreline's black
Bread
Forgive
Our bodies shivering
Us our debts
Hands dumb and white
As we forgive
At the misery whip
Our debtors
Back and forth sawing
Breathing shuddering temptation
Deliver us
Felling your favorite tree

Loam

for Reba

with her sister gone, she tends to her
garden,
    gentle in the failing
        light of dusk
      feeling alive, loose in her bones
        lovely in her gray
      hair, her memories,
          dirt under her
            fingernails

fire of the sun soon
        gone still, shimmering in the waving
trees
      burning in her eyes
        nourishing the vines, a lone vigilant Reba
rose,
      the hopes of bloom.

(should I say something and
interrupt her meditation,
her quiet time in her backyard
garden – no more than that –
interrupt her being her.)

wetness smells, of her garden
        awakening for its
      nightly desire at full stretch

reaching up to cup her
chin, to rest on her shoulders
the promise
the promise of
solace once again in living
things,
well-tended, loved.

she moves with full knowledge
there is a God
of things that
grow at night
in the unseen
light,
there is a darkness we all
must harvest
to eat of the plentiful
to consume
and return
from loam, to
loam
one family; a variety of plants,
a sister returned
to the garden.

she discards weeds and brushes tears from her cheeks
standing in the near dark
of following seasons.

Garage / Sale

1.
Better than a sundial
Tables at a garage sale

2.
She turns over glass, reads
          History painted by factory workers
Long ago on her family farm
          Running through the living
Room chasing invisible birds
          Shaking the wood floor with footfalls
Thunder, rattling cats and china
To the unforgiving floor to scatter
          Memory
One more inexplicable
          Shard

3.
One lines leads
          To another
Sometimes parallel and other
          Times round
Universes and confusions –
          Dilemma both personal
Historical and flat
          Out
Boundless

4.

The porch swing does not sway
Now lying on the grass for sale
Cut down from its ropey mooring
Swingers long gone
Down the road a little
Unbalanced

5.

Beneath the knitted skull cap
A bald head
Her teeth the hue of cold tea
She walks the yard
Touching this plant and that green
Thing saying matter-
Of-factly – *this is hardy*
This will last

4:47

In this house, on this morning… Forty-three fountain-pens, pots of purple ink (Virginia Woolf before the stones), some with blue-black (my bruises in proses); fourteen manual typewriters, the elder statesman an Underwood Standard #6 built in January 1935… a library of over four hundred books; Leo Tolstoy, Frederick Buechner, Meister Eckhart, all within easy reach alongside a psalter… There are groaning shelves of journals dating back to 1987 where in a journal page I have stuck a perfectly-peeled beer bottle label (which meant you were a virgin) … Dogs are barking, Mr. Coffee beeping; be right back. muse, be right… *I can't read your mind…* Music plays, always, mostly classical (lunatic Scriabin, mystical Dmitri Dmitriyevich Shostakovich, the brilliant Philip Glass) and jazz when I'm writing, lyrical when I'm freewriting — every morning the same sentence begins my day *in this house, on this morning, — Even tho I'm here I'm already gone* And I write in some purple ink anything at all that comes into my mind, so that when I come to my typewriter I can hit the keys running, so that when… *Our shadows remain even after we are gone* I sit down with HAL I get the words off Qwerty and onto the page and then… *I will write it in the sky, baby…* and today is today, and wherever you go there you are…*already gone*…and then…

(4:47 "Even Tho" by Joseph Arthur)

Ahead of Me

Just as the sun rises Venus is in transit
Across the blaze a tiny speck of dust
Centuries in celestial making kismet
On a day when I see the sun at its palest.
Four years ago, this day you left us
Vibrating to a different distant measure
With little but mystery dripping from our hands
What to do with them now, at sunrise.
Looking up there in the draining dark of morning
I want to see you as more than dust
You were my future, the one full of wonder and warning
Ahead of me in age, the family's shyest.
As that black speck rides fire
I send a prayer to long my mourning
This transit rare, beautiful and ephemeral
It is not our last conversation, brother.
For you are still ahead of me, racing across the sun.
Wonder and warning in your run.

Meditating with Jigsaw

for Jane K.

Jigsaw is upside down
and on the table
I scratch under her chin
and feel blessed the day
is breaking noon noise
the woodlands alive
with bird cantos high
of workmen humming
I had been feeling
low for not meditating
but with the cat's soft murmur
blissful eyes, I was given
over to a satori
the enlightenment there sat
in the noon making sound
I had indeed been here
me, meditating with one
of its masters who purrs as
if sighing a joyful: *Om.*

She Carries Irises

She carries irises
Back seat of her borrowed get-a-way car
Holding the wheel, nothing of his

No destination but seeking far abeyances
In with ardent thrown longing
She carries irises

Driving until she's escaped history
Over bridges and familiar roads
Holding the wheel, nothing of his

Head and heart sung stung with wishes
New found beauty far away
She carries irises

Her Father says carry love on every hegira
Never knowing exactly where you're going
Holding the wheel, nothing of his

Loose threads her life through
Hope of starting new
Holding the wheel, steering now His
She carries irises

Tomorrow Song

If tomorrow were songs
        we'd be singing till our throats were hoarse
        shortly before morning comes into the cantus firmus
        light burning low, eyes misty, hands numb
        on the kitchen table,
        resting near tumblers of tears,
                watching dawn chew away the chorus,
        our throats straining for justice.
        Oh, tomorrow, come as if a song.

Blood into Wine

Toilet water baptism in a bus depot
after we slept in the graveyard, still
no one goes there at night, and
by day they think we're lingering ghosts.
But we have been Christened parsons
torn flesh on our own way of sorrow
realized fourteen stations of the cross
soup kitchen sacraments, where we
hear the beatitudes, chanted psalms,
vespers prayers lining out bedroll, our
drunken reveries, confessional scream
seeking amid the debris, the returned
who walks on water, provider of alcohol
man, who bleeds rust and dirt from behind
a rock, the center of his palms, clutching
at the light, the wine bottle, his thorny
crown in the cemetery on the knoll of trees
where we slumber and murmur midrash
amidst the windswept sandstone, watching
vandals clip angels topple memories
to a legion of martyrs, one married
ones given to the soul, covered, and drenched
in sorrow, inebriated with repose, relief
here waiting, inoculated against rapture
scanning tombstone for the calling of home
His return,
the return of His
blood into wine.

Blue Thread

You are there long after being gone
Standing as if nothing happened.
Holding out your moonlit hand
A blue thread to hold.

Only in morning do I speak—
Thread, I croak, still half asleep.
It was blue. Upstairs we go search
You're not there, of course.

But for the thread, stitched in the sun
Blue, of course, blue thread.
What other color would it be?

Again, Born

For Lindsay

Though you can't understand
Yet peace by an imposition of hands
Though you can't feel
Yet Trinity anointing a soul tattoo
Though you can't see
Yet Sacrament of the Seal bestowing grace
It is confirmed on days of bread and wine
Confirmed with headwaters, and intercession
Affirming you, again, perfect
Again, born, perfect Christian
Though you can't believe you were born
Perfect, an ancient rite speaks of it,
The Holy Spirit dwells inside
Vessels only made of pure light

Things to Do This Fall

First, I must take off the old, decaying boards
they are splitting and warping, spitting nails
Then I need to measure them so I can go to the lumber store;
knowing exactly what I need I will tell them I need
To re-caulk the exterior wall, filling those darkened gaps
I will ask my neighbor for a long ladder, to reach them

Back home I will place the new boards on with nails
making sure the decking is secure and fixed to the foundation
I will hammer in nails until I dent the wood with my stroke
I may paint over the gaps, re-apply water resistant to the wood—
I do all this slowly. If I hurry I get frustrated, make mistakes;
there is no quality in haste, simply the job gets done

It does not last; things let go, if I let them
I must summon the courage to do the job
I am afraid of myself
of my lack of will, my ability to ignore what
is right in front of me, letting go
perhaps then I can fully mourn my dead brother

Perhaps then I can see that he is gone
even when I saw that he was getting old and decaying
I stood on that rusted nail I'd meant to take care of
and let my foot bleed
I did nothing—
for fear of myself

Bone in the Belly

Bone in the belly
Bird bellow above
What has happened here?
In the garden, nest upturned.

Two inexplicable beaks crying
The cat, my cat, is in the wicked splendor
Using a drawn umbrella, I enter the fray.

Lifting one, then another fragile miracle
Up, back into the safety of trees
Their wildness remains in my palms
Standing back to view the rescue.

My heart beats in rhythmic reminder
Preciousness is the purview of God
It is difficult to rid the memory
Even though we don't know what that looks like.

Mother mockingbird stares blankly
It is as if she missed it; that I don't exist
Drawing down the umbrella
Taking leave their devil in my care.

Days feed on grub worm and thunderstorms
An empty nest brings me a fluted glory
Still, I wonder of their flight
Is it far away or merely nearby, hiding?

The cat, my cat, listless and drooling
X-rays show what it looks like
In his ghostly inferno belly, inside
There, an echo of bellowing birds.

Bone in the belly
How can I let bad things happen?
Banish such beauty from the garden
When their wildness is still in my palms?

Review End Year

As a gift, this old calendar
mailed, addressed, not discarded
assigned a place, through an arrangement
of days and night of old, sealed
to be opened and examined from afar
perhaps discussed, mulled over wine
each day marked by verification, hues
colors fading, gone yet present
mailed, addressed, not discarded to
yourself, a gift of many days and
nights, hovering over each day, pencil erasure
in midair, verifying the year that was
accounting for the beginning, recording
the middle and denying I was ever there.

By

Field scorched by fire. Water dried by the sun.

by

God, by, by,

the sun

scorched

by fire, by God, dried

why must I ponder

searing death, water, by fire

reflective, by by

God, scorching,

dried by the field of my ravenous beating

fire-red heart,

when water dried by the sun. Blackness covers,
reigns, crowned

with

fresh snow

new water. Sun and man

melting and returning to

by   by God. By God. Oh my.

What have we done?

Constellation

A constellation of possibilities
blinking
            soft needs, soft deeds
a nightfall summer breeze
heavy with water beneath
                        the trees
pondering the mechanics of
                        drifting
friends, boats
                        and thoughts.
There, over Orion
arching, being acted upon, back
towards a black hole
her name, her fragrance,
                        her Cassiopeia face
slipping from consciousness
distant as a dying star
breezing towards seamless
oblivion
feigning boats
thoughts
this hand outstretched in a half gesture
a wave goodbye in the
                        dark.

Suburban Silence

Eleven twenty —
Silences surround numb houses
In farmer's furrows of long gone seasons
Now row upon straight row. Vinyl white picket
Fences, thin trees, mark virgin grasses

Blue sky —
High hawk singing its wings
Over where not a solitary soul
Accompanies me through the noonday
Light. Every house a Hopper scene

Empty —
Yet beautifully lit.
For shadows duet with the sun
The ballad of what's yet to come
Beyond eleven twenty-one.

Five Storeys

You hanging out the apartment window calling out to me spring in the Village, the promise of warmer weather maybe I should have stopped, there on the sidewalk, just a moment turned my face to you five storeys above, shielded my eyes of the sun just a moment, to stop amid the traffic, the change of season to catch your gaze, your words floating slowly to the ground where I should have stood, motionless, palms turned upward, hopeful instead hurrying to work, your voice joined the city symphony of spring my head contemplating work, a coming season, love with you in a world five storeys above the midst of it all.

Running

While running, I found a hand
Tiny and plastic palm up
It read: *Love me—*
Take it for a sign
From someone watching nearby
Or far resumed my pace
Knowing a wait was now upon
Me as all great answers
Require continual running
Toward an indiscriminate vanishing
Point where all mysteries go to be reckoned.

Random Abstract

Harmony bell between my breasts,
                    a secret shimmer, jitters,
rests.

photo, black and white, and me, from '66 taped to the cottage
                    window, '77 newspaper account of a probe on
the floor shall I include this frozen refrain,
                    this smile yet to know pain?

the indecipherable language of whales,
                    a Peruvian wedding song.
my random abstracts,
                    on morphine, defeat
                              diluted heartbeat.

to remain hidden is to survive,
                    seamonsterCharybdismychestbonefire
latent with harmony bells ringing
                    waves, wine-dark bird swooping, singing.

Blind Willie Johnson's slide guitar, blues
                    Navajo night chants, the Voyager cries, coos
please contact,
                         please contact, please...
on the way of black milk, where muted, diseased,

distant my singular star dies.
such sweetness,
the trumpeting bellow of elephants,
the baying of wild dogs,
sleep over songs, poems
this black and white me, before a secret illness
when they come, when they contact, relentless,
regardless, passionless, me no more, no less.

all that floating in the black ocean
Hawking's Time
but me young now, than I was
older, then...
the secrets they will not know, rendered irrelevant, end.

Please contact,
please contact,
before these bones snap, dry cinder sighs,
harmony bells, morphine fugues, vacant eyes.

what part of me
goes
with a heavy vine of grapes for wine?

what part of me,
goes into this satellite speeding billions of eons away
to this life form
afar?

what part of me,
rests, lies,
with lost friends, filling their heads
with country roads, drunken joyrides, birthday cards,
inner city dead-ends?

what part of me Carl Sagan?
please contact.

are *you* there?
beneath my absent nipple, my phantom breast
the waves, the nausea
the stars,
the rest?

this synonymous purpose. Two Voyagers, three including me.
All seeking to cross the river why,
accepting, the torrents of this black ocean wide.

Please contact,
fading fast in
dying light

walking itself back to slag, tongues
stilled, the taste of rust.

Came here,
to smell damp grass, the lodge pole pine
beneath the latent dust, a little girl stood alone

not wanted on the probe,
not to be contacted.

while screaming silent falls,
my secret roams, installs.

to remain hidden is to survive
walking
back to soil, sunrise
they will not show, to our vacant eyes
the secrets, that shimmer, jitters
and rests, and dies
consuming its hosts, long retired from sentry posts.

at last, and then,
frail fingers flounder for a movement in the skin
straining to push forth, to rally cries,
to acquire the indecipherable language of whales.
please contact.

Rebuild

Storms level our pale shelters
We rebuild that's what we do.
We gather what we can—
Doors never stepped through,
Windows without panes,
Stairs with broken steps,
Lamps and linens folded into our arms.
We stand where we once were,
Begin again we survive harm—
The driveway, the stoop, the door
Lock and key.
Soon, all has been restored,
Houses stand strong again we stand
Strong, our love raising these shelters.
We all know to do otherwise would be wrong,
That our building is made sturdier
Only by borrowing
By lending a hand
To others, torn, not defeated
Broken not busted,
Neighbors not strangers.
That's what we do
We rebuild that's what we do.
Rebuild ourselves through each other.

Pepper's Ghost

Align the mirror just so, the angle is key
To see again, unlock created bodies —
A duality of sensitivity and strength —
Remembrance of her sway and lines
Everything night, she often said, over tea and cigarettes
I have something to do, and if not, I make something
To do with the reflection of what once was important
I wanted to tell her she need not explain
Least of all to me, holding the consideration so
Yet I saw now that she did need
To have it said perhaps once if not a thousand
Times as she stirred her tea, and lit another
Cigarette its length the weight of time and attention
Applying her makeup and telling me it was all
A disguise, sonny boy, and winked

Levaya

In honor of Lew and Bill

Waif paper thin men and their scorched lovers
Exeunt with dustbins and all those ashes to disperse.
Alone but for a while surrounded by filaments
Tied to remembering moments, flickering briefly.
All coming to unfurl over the earth, the water as dust—
Don't talk to me—
Eventually all but gone in the end, save
It is not good for man to be alone—
Someone, a doula, levaya, capturing that last backward glance
Don't talk to me—
A look, I was here I've done my time
Don't forget to stow away the dustbin,
Let down the fire escape with great care.
Now, *Stay with me, stay with me—*
Until it is all out.

Succor Drawn

Intuitive butterflies tend tears
Icarus moths dare challenge flame
Seven-year cicadas dream dark loam
Myriad mysteries without clues—
Hummingbird
Handwritten, sent in a single note
To you, quite unexpectedly
Opening coda to new lacunae
Laws drawn by unyielding science.
—Birds swooping glass for open sky.

Daedalus' Wings

If Daedalus' wings were available,
the sun weakened, cornered,
then perhaps the dead
would bury its dead in due time
and the weak-pulsed princess, frozen
in paparazzi
would ascend
the booze-filled Mercedes tank
twisted, infested with crawling ants
flashing police sirens, tiaras compacted
in airbags
lifting her Raggedy-Anne broken body
and up
towards the sun again,
once and for all private, and yet,
lilies on her casket,
in an overwhelmed abbey,
where she once held court,
but (the world's cruelest turn)
wax cannot withstand
scrutiny, the speed of machines
once the vessel for light
became
darkness and its hindrance,
beneath the city

of lights,
Daedalus loses yet another who
sought the sun
but (cruelty again)
was burnt by its flash, its intensity,
the photographer, a German named Rat,
held her limp wrist,
and felt nothing, but what he thought
what he tried to forget feeling, witnessing

was not only struggling flight
in the absence of wings, but
also, the sight of a single feather,
floating, down, down, towards
the sullen earth.

Embalming a King

King Sikkim is in the lotus position, and quite dead.

His swollen feet are gently tucked beneath him and in a knot. Dust on his idle hands, now. Motionless chanting for sun, deftly murmuring the name of his favorite toy, dreaming blithely of a fleshly Gaia. Smelling of the West, in alchemy of sweet oil and dollar bills. Stilled coins in his pocket. Those expecting to witness his bloodletting, suffer and reconsider finality's housekeeping. The Japanese travel in hermetically sealed airplanes and limousines to jot notes and pencil diagrams. Peer over dark glasses. Dignitaries, puzzle with the indignity. The dead must look dead, right?

Viewing before a descent into hell. Sikkim dances with Greta Garbo, Judy Garland with blood on her toes, in the exodus spiral. Judy belts out. Bulging throat veins.

For King Sikkim, there was no ceremonial tug. No ankle hold. No opportunity to turn the reign upside down causing coins to fall onto the off-gray, cold floor of the New York embalmer where all sentences end without repeal.

All periods. For golden kings and silver screen sirens. All dark for the leather looks southward, with eyelids flapped shut, over grieving, ironic, well-wishers who shudder with flaring nostrils.

Oh, that's how they do it. It is how the king wanted it. Only in North America is one embalmed. He wanted eternity with Garbo.

Somehow the box is closed, the ground brought closer. Grass concludes the praying over King Sikkim, in a contemplative manner.

Quite dead.

Sandwiches are served for those who continue to shake their heads in disbelief.

Strange Land

Fridays for falling
To our knees, blind. Modern world under laws
Smoked on miracles thousands of years old.
Now, watching sublimated starlings swoop
Cerulean sky. You ask: *What's good now*
About an execution? Perhaps what
Uplifts we cannot know. The heart inert
Stone moving. Corpus felt more than seen. Death
For life. Blood coursing through—propinquity
Forgiven, washed, blessed here. Understanding
What's crime. What's salvation—witness, comes
Again, unexpectedly fluttering
Birds. Anything of transcendent beauty
Patience requires a waiting that aches and
Tests. Waiting is rewarded with a cry
So deep its bursting is thousands of years
Building suddenly again. I answer:
Our strange land blood is made of iron and wine.

Nodding over Coffee

For Ron

Nodding over coffee hungering dark
Alighting murder of crows making way
To whispering wires strung
Pole to pole humming fractured
Discourse of a strange land held together
With apologies, affirmations, alibis
Things unseen but felt in our bonefires lit
Kindling rolled up pages from the message passed
Hand to hand during the raven ravages of war
Known by two old friends, talking over
Their brew as loneliness
Whose appetite wanes, thirst slaked by
Nodding over coffee
Together
Yet miles from one
Another's matin prayer...

Quaker Bardo

.

.

.

.

.

.

.

.

.

Feel the peace
One hundred seconds to here
Ninety-nine names for the unsayable.

Outside Emporia

A row of crucifixes cut through the nervous evermore-
colored in hues of blood, money, memory, and redemption.
Voices carry over the whisper wires; a murder of crows.
Thank Christ, we don't live here, — but we do. This is the
world's longest, continuous memory. From the churning sea
of generation, to the wine-dark ocean of good-byes, where
forever laps and sighs, we must always pass through God's
desolate middle ground.

Everywhere sin without direction, furrows for the
blind, junegrass saint fenceposts and sheltering sky. We
conjure blonde blades of grass, leaves of a book, recall failed
correspondence, ponder wonder whys — there're no songs
about the middle of the road, the middle of this country,
where crucifixes line the road through God's domain.

Where in the stillness,

only a murmur, the flapping of wings.

Me & Mary Oliver

It matters not
                        The right edge
Turns by vibration, sounds
                        Breaking
& every break ushering a turn
                        Every day a line
Heads back in the direction
                        It came
Stresses, taps toe nervously
                        Listens, scans
Often lightly, then heavily
                        Upon
Echoes of light / heavy,
                        Light / heavy, light /
Heavy, light / heavy,
                        Light / heavy
Paradise Lost, As You
                        Like It
Prelude to Frost
                        All lines
Of breath
                        Ineffable
Heavy lifting
                .   Lightly
Shared

Neighborhood of Prayer

The unknown is our blessing and burden
All we have is this present moment
We travel in neighborhoods anew
Maybe scared, uncertain, enlightened
By the possibilities of residing there
Fully denizens of the burden
More attuned, blessed of the open future
Slowly driving down unfamiliar lanes
Where we would live if only
The days and nights unrolled, parched
As our answered prayers

Engine of Pride

Cold, white, empty; a timepiece sits on the nearby mantle. The visitor awakens, the head of King Kong lifts from the pillow: Where is everyone? Last night slips through the curtain and out in the break of day over old album covers, garage sale knickknacks, paddy whacks, no dog, know how, to give a bone in this crypt. The visitor, about to stir, senses the cold, but has no other option. He places his white feet on the hardwood, dull, scuffed floor and examines the place he has ended up. He thinks of trains, the train he once was. Now a rail. Put a penny on his back. This was not the plan to wake up alone, the temporary best friends gone, and the sun of another day playing on his thick head. No, this was not the plan. He walks to the mantle to find the quarter-size pocket watch dead, the engine of pride, in his alcohol-bloated hands, dead. He ponders theft, but then no. He is a rail, they placed a penny on his back, and these temporary friends have been kind to the roaming drunk. Instead, yes, there's always instead, he winds the timepiece after setting its tiny hands right. He winds it and leaves, without a note, a brief good-bye. The engine of pride ticks on, he can hear it as he walks barefoot down the early morning street, seeking inclusion.

A man needing help with a fence.
A gardener and her roses.
A boy and his ball.
Anything to stop him for a moment, to halt the ticking in his head.
Instead, there's always instead.
This cold, white emptiness where his bare feet take him.

Sober

A great cure for worry
in a blade of grass
desire in full stretch,
green, reedy, tossing
lightly in the wind
where the worry has
alighted, swept asunder
a sober awakening
oddly too, a drifting away
unburdened by confusion
immersed
baptized, reborn clean,
sober.

The Ocean at Night

Our bodies are anchors
lowered by reluctant angels
these are their fluttering kites
it comes with such a splash
of light, such bursts of song
the thrown bodies, the flying
thoughts.

This is where the universe
comes at the unbearable
speed of light staining
your soul, making the heart
an instrument of unpredictability
that is when we come to feel
absence in another anchor
once owned by hesitating
seraphim.

We are forged, thrown
grown in a bone, drone
moan motherhood—
then and thereafter,
our thoughts, our fingers
fumble for kite strings,
the anchor chain, the source
of such here and now
breathlessness—

Unbearable umbrage—
unimaginably holy
our fingernails, thin, brittle
optic nerves, razor—
sharp like death
night has grown while we
sleep and sway upon
the ocean.

We believe in time, but we
feign ghosts.

Why Fences

Her heart was heavy as she took to the farm road, the slack rein dangling in her hand. She watched her unsteady feet, her leather shoes, grow dusty in the crunching gravel. She had moved here because he asked when others did not. She felt like such a city girl. About a mile from the farm, she was breathless and thirsty. Her ears filled with wind and emptiness. The open gate came to her and she dismissed it; she placed the coarse rope around the pole: secure, right? He had told her to keep her penned. *That's what the fence is for, to keep out the wide open spaces,* he had said. Too deep in her thoughts, she did not hear the car coming. A human's voice saying, *Excuse me*, made her turn. It was a man, East Indian perhaps, standing at the side of his car, the door ajar. *I'm lost.* She walked to the car, *Where were you going?* Hearing her own voice, dry and ragged, surprised her. She cleared her throat, gulped in the hot summer air. A hand went up to comb her hair, but she stopped herself. What would be the use out here? *I don't know, really.* She blinked and stopped at the front of the car. *I don't know how to get there.* He laughed. *Sorry; I am a bit preoccupied: the horses.* Even in the heat, she felt a shiver. *The horses?* she looked about; her own horse was missing from her pen. He pointed at the horizon. *Did you see them?* The farmer's wife shook her head. *Three of them, well, two; one got hit over there. I have been following them for half an hour, down one country road after another. I thought they were loose and then when Amtrak... Are those reins? Is one of the horses yours?* She looked dumbly at the leather strap in her clean, white hand. *She's missing.* He pointed. *They're coming back, see.* She turned. Two faint dots shimmered through the waves of heat on the horizon. She squinted: Could it be her? That horse meant everything to her—it sickened her to think it was dead. It was such a wild thing; you could see it in her eyes. The vastness of the prairies made her heart ache; why fences? She wanted so badly for her horse to be alive there on the horizon running free, its nostrils drinking in the watery heat. As the two animals neared, she whistled and one horse stopped, briefly; cantering. She could hear nothing but her own breathing now. She thought about the idling car, and the man standing there. *Where are you going?* she wanted him to ask. The reins in her hands felt like dry rope. The open gate came to her. The horse cantered as if thinking. *I don't know how to get there.*

The Pole of Relative Inaccessibility

We are puer aeternus and puella aeterna
We live at the pole of most trouble, the pole of relative inaccessibility
The middle of nowhere in metaphysics
Simply we have a large yard, but no fence – yet
We are neither here nor there, past nor present, young nor old,
Amidst the abyss, a physics teacher with no limbs once told us
My wings have been dipped in wax, her cheeks brushed with ash
I have a cut on my thigh, she gets cramps
We live from check to check
Me and her and a cat named Jigsaw
She wants to play the saxophone
Jigsaw wants to bound and roll
I want to reassemble the broken down bicameral brain
We have friends who are married and have kids
We have friends who are not married and have kids
We want kids, we have no kids ourselves
Most of the time we wish we had kids of our own
We have no money, really, but we have a car, some furniture
A stereo that plays jazz real smooth, and a computer
I write longhand and drink scotch
I work in front of a computer all day eating lunch with a doppelgänger
Of Buckminster Fuller and we talk about decahedrons
We are no longer in school, we're not into our careers yet
I wonder where J.D. Sunset is?
We have old friends in terms of their age, we have young friends

We have no friends our own age – 27 and 24
Jigsaw is a billion years' old
We moved a few years ago from the north, to the south, and then west
We plan to move West again in one year
We are not gypsies – we believe trees only grow roots
When about to be pushed over
I miss a certain English teacher who rolled his own cigarettes
Smuggled cocaine into Baja
And now, only has one lung
She wishes her mum would move closer
We are somewhat confused
Cry while sitting on the toilet
And in the shower in the morning
We laugh when it's least expected
Smile generally most of the time
Why not?
We want a house, a garden, a place to stack books
And address with the torn-out pages
Architectural Digest, Home
And Gardens strewn about
We want freedom from an ordinary, time-wasting life
We're after a sensory-filled life in a house
In a meadow, near water
At night, we dress like housewives
And rob 7-Eleven Stores at gunpoint
We put the stolen money in paper bags
As we drive, as we make our get-a-way, we throw the bag
Out the window as we go over a bridge in strange parts

Of the city, we live by
We tell stories to cats in Hebrew
We search back alleys for black holes
We charted a route to Lyndon, Washington
From New Orleans
Underground
I've a degree in Sociology
I learned about men and women
She's a business major, learning how to run
Things
Jigsaw is a reincarnated Buddhist monk
We may retire to Tibet
Or Asteroid B-612
We have a dying Fuchsia plant on our balcony
She can get pregnant at the drop of a hat
I have three hats
One brown, two straw
I have a cap from Scotland
We are madly in love
Always have been always will be, we shall
Never part
Divorce is something other people do
Recently she found a paper bag full of money
We bought Jigsaw a new dish
We have solved the mystery of the deep loch
Pyramids and the Bermuda Triangle
We have snapshots
We have fingerprints
We drink spearmint tea and read A.A. Milne

Mortgages stump us
Our bank manager has a black moustache and wear track suits
He's nameless, and walks with a limp
I once wanted to be an actor
I once wanted to be John Wayne
She used to want to save the world
She is still trying to save the world
With hot water bottles
And black and white Carey Grant movies
We are talented
But shy
I love jazz
Movies, reading and walking
She loves all this and more
I love her
She is afraid of a lot of
Things
I am curious about a lot of
Things
I know what she's afraid of
We don't stock our shelves with any
As children, we laid a plank across a ditch
To walk across the chasm
Played marbles, hid in trees, got pocket money
Every Friday of the week
People thought us popular
Fate brought us together
I found Jigsaw under a truck
Her hair all full of oil

She rode seven miles by the engine
From a farm
And lived
She and I travel by plane – and like it
We love Jigsaw
And Jigsaw loves us
Things have gotten so complicated
Sitting in a café, summer heat coming
Down
I think about that
Catch me if I fall
We used to say
We hold hands, encourage, give messages
Rub temples
Go on walks and look at other people's homes
We write letters
To friends we haven't seen
Since the third grade
We write simply
You are missed
Love
We never sign our names
We watch movies and cry together
We know what a misery whip is
The future is a vanishing
Point we realize
We are walking
It is okay

We are not alone
Jigsaw is trailing
ACK-ACK
She has no vocal chords
Born that way
There's a ditch!
Get a plank!
Hold hands
Smile
Cry
We are aeternus
Aeterna
We love one another
Crossing makes us dizzy
She carries Jigsaw
Tomorrow we make clouds
Into whales and tall ships
And plan to ask
Julia Roberts over
For spearmint tea
We are getting older
The sun closer
The clock has restless hands
Catch us if we
Fall

Stones

Response to Sirens

Sailor lost at sea
Sirens calling out to me—

Singing you, humming me
The way truth conforms to music
Low voices carry over deceiving seas
Enchanting fandango; fidelity exalted
Response to Sirens—
Averting rocks, shipwreck and beguiling brine
We sing of the salt, of the unsated thirst
We celebrate not the singers,
The singing, the singing luscious
Cantus firmus fateful lust
Tied to a mast drowsy tossing
Drunk boat listing over wine-dark deep
Song of myself, for myself, by myself
Unable, unwilling, to box my ears
—No, not drowning, singing to drown you out.
Can you kittiwakes not hear me?
Squawking your incessant score
One man alone left warbling fantod
Past bleached skulls beached at your tapping talons

Tattoos

Tattoo battered pendulum arms
Of the things he's seen
Blue birds and tangled webs
Vines and dark angels on Harleys.

Back and forth his arms the
Hue of hope, descant, memory
Part flesh, part art.

Air, arms pumping
ahead of him, as a
constant reminder of
the things he's seen
and where he's been.

Mother, then
Loverlines
Then, Mother
Loverlines

Turning slightly, I see at the center of his chest
Sliced with dye, a crucified Christ,
His back, a Chagall canvas where
The winds whip welts, wounds, worn
The things that are behind
Him, part flesh, part art.

He stares ahead as he cuts a swath
Through the beauty of the lilies,
Picassos serendipity tracks mutilating his inner
Arms, pumping, self-abusive, reborn
Through the passage of the day,
The poison slowly dripping off his fingertips.

Unharvested in furrows

We are gypsies of no fixed redress
weakened instruments of commerce
immigrants of liberty, purveyors of weightlessness
feigners of maps and hometowns
offering meager opinions and vague recollections
we are Ulysses on the skirt of nullification
we strive, seek, to find a shift in geography
a sense of place in our marrow-bones
we create clouds of dust at our heels
and wear compasses for watches
we are Johnny Appleseed leaving ourselves
freshly planted, moist, easily uprooted
unharvested in furrows of local yore, our names
specks, spent matches, grain
we only go back one generation, one season
there are few surviving photo albums
no line to king nor homecoming queen
minions in a million march of meanings
we remember, but are forgotten
footprints in eroding silt, retraced rivets
reading our history one foot at a time
biography a collection of washboard roads
blacktop and gray, snaking concrete lineage
impenetrable itinerary leading up over
the away, constant searching for an entrance
into the soft folds of belonging.

Slow Lone Burn

He leaves

The scent of Cameroon wrappers grown in the shade, the sound of *Leaves Of Grass, Love Among The Ruins,* read to him while rolling cigars in the thighs of a virgin for Ernest Fuente's in the Dominican Republic; or for Angel Olivia, Sr, in Brazil, a season of rain; Ybor City just after the Havanas were snuffed out.

Roll, move, leaves, light:

Still there, years later even in Connecticut, where the winters are cold, the ember of his choices burning brighter, finite. Never stay in one place long enough, to record a voice muddied with dialect, register a face in the familiar parade of features, instead listen to the different tongues speak poetry, tell lies or give advice while nodding over coffee. Luggage heavy with memories, but easy to shoulder. Rust colored, leathered, but unexpectedly manicured hands press fat cigars into his breast pocket, a hushed monosyllabic word; a humidor door shuts, rotating ceiling fan. Hands, on his lap, numb, repose with regret. That lone bulb dangling.

Roll, move, leaves, light:

First hesitant steps away. Ash dust on the top of his boots. Roll fifty coronas before crossing the border in the Nicaraguan dawn; the bus depot, smelling of urine, in

Rock Springs, Montana near the glowing gold mine, a black man disappears behind the veil of a Montecristo, a Zino and confesses political murder; a hoarfrost-cold Vancouver, B.C. morning behind a forgotten dilapidated hotel, without currency, but rich within the aroma of his constant companions: El Rico Habana; Davidoff; Primo Del Rey, forms in the smoky shadows; oh, the stories they weave. Not, *Stand up straight, Keep your head about you, Get outta town,* swirling around crowding plans, hopes and routes, but no, the haste choices made, faint spice smoke obscures memory, flavors recollection, his face covered by a numbing curtain of sorrow, fumes a landmine map to weary eyes, of the ever mutable road beyond, the path littered with broken, spent, wooden matches; ashtray conversations with old, disappearing friends and family.

Roll, move, leaves, light:

His fire, his resolution for a home, a place for his body, a grave, as tenuous as slag in a slight breeze. This sojourn endures, wrapping itself in shade, in the rough edges of mystery, an orange mesmerizing filament in the abyss, where the only constant is gone, the only future burning away in rapturous moments suffuse with a million gracious images of her and him, them and they, in his ruinous hands, unexpectedly smelling of Cameroon wrappers, of poetry, this slow lone burn.

Leaves, light:

Fingertips yet unsinged, fumble for a light in the heavy dark of his inertia, this imposed gravity. Inhale, move, roll.

Wrapped around both a sentence and a phantom is a desire.

Burn ember, burn. Finds himself near Unity, skulking in a thicket of rust and alibis.

Ash on his teeth.

Leaves.

The Line

In the juggle of twist and salvation
We know hate, we know death
Always air thick with fear, the arid smell
Pain rising a fist with every sun.
Scrolls and tracts are fingered, messiahs
Messages presaged, foretold, forewarned.
What is written in hefty stone—
This is my house, get out; try and move it.
This is my land, step off; try to move me.
Stasis umbilicus paper and fire. Blood.
What is rare, is lightness when all is
Grievous and inconsolable—
Levity in a ferocious line
Of sand and people in a Middle Eastern dust
Storm. Of Jews on one side
Palestinians bluster on the other.
Each erasing with stubborn boots
The line. Crossing each other on the
Way seldom meeting. Never seeing each other
Eye to eye.
Each speaking their Deity's tongue
Language of loss buried deep belief—
This is the land of a thousand generations
Suns rising over fields of blood feud. And yet—
Visited by three supermodels, on a photo
Shoot, near a newly erected barrier more
Than 450 miles long. Centuries sunk.

Leaning haughtily neutral in couture glad
Rags beneath a flourish of Arabic graffiti.
Nearby Allah schoolboys snicker, point all knowingly—
Not at exposed cleavage as one would expect, but at
The script coming as plainly as Quranic verse:
I am a Big Donkey.
Mute models sashay while a photographer continues
The shooting.

Erratics

no immortal stone
left unturned

the erractics lumbering dumb
prairie field postcards

from an age of ice.
I seek to comprehend where

sin comes from?
Snakes, apples, arrows

falling short of their target.
A lone stone,

rolling alone, for me
to touch, to taste.

Why not sin?
where there is silence, surrounded

by emptiness
left from another time

pushed and abandoned.
Surrounded by sinister ssssnakessss

radioactive crucifixes
a worn path leading away

back into the car.
My breathing appearing,

vanishing on the window
as if never there at all.

Immortal stones turned,
left to erode in silence.

The Grendel Considerations

Yes, Grendel is upset
The Geats and their racket
Wergild, comitatus
Great hall great mess
Never did it cross their minds
The unquiet disturbs him
And yet, he pauses to consider
Yoga! How it could turn his life around
Probiotic diets, Norwegian string quartets
Proust by dusk's golden candlelight
Amid their drunken clamor their singing
Swords and persistent shouting
Stopping dead his sun salutations, his thoughts
About moving to Wellsville, Kansas
And storms their party instead, slewing
Scores of them, severing arms, sinking
Jagged fangs into jugulars, smashing
The hall's Ikea furnishings into splinters
Never did it cross their minds
To keep it down, just a smidgen, to
Perhaps, send him an invitation
Join us —
Even if it was: *bring a lawn chair*
BYOB
Never did it cross their minds

He is lonely and sought friends
He lives with his mother, so heartbreaking!
Their card could have read simply —
Join us and to a man
Tell us where
Your suffering began

Silent Syllables

The day of the parade—
Folk huddled beneath chattering insect trees
Noisily humming themselves, dismantling metal instruments
Hopscotch lines smeared on cracked pavement
The red prophesy fading, alarming crying children
Parade of muttering war veterans and yawning auto mechanics
Hoisting rusty tools, spent engines, flags unfurled flapping
Brass bands following crashing cymbals
As work and plates of food clatter continue unabated
Gorging bone and meat until the blackened clouds came, scattering all
Screaming indoors sealing themselves off drawing thick curtains
Shutting out rattling noise of expected thunder
Wiping clean smudges and unrequited grins
Everyone silent briefly, eyes closed, tight strict rows
Preparing to doubt then symphonically hissing skeptically
—As the word moved into the neighborhood
Transmogrifying sibilants into silent syllables of grace
Even the insects halted in wonder
As resplendent rain fell without a sound.

Muted Fury

You don't want to talk about it
if we did
        you'd beat my chest
        throw back
                your head.
I know you should have
                told me
        could have listened
        cupped an ear to
                your breastbone
spoke about the
                weight,
        the unbearable,
                the unsustainable
        could have taken sadness
                from your hair
        tangled and wind torn
                still feeling fingers
fists, knuckles,
                the past.
Instead,
                we stare
        at the remains

of the day   spilling

onto the floor

away from us

feet,

carrying on its back

our stillness,

our muted fury.

Umbrage

Another suburban spring sunrise. Empty
Of reckless blooming. Everywhere
Manicured lawns introduce tidy houses.
Trimmed bracken subtly acknowledges
Our ability to keep nature at bay.
From the recently-stained deck I watch
My cat skulks across the verdant carpet
Sneak up on a cardinal
Clamp the startled bird in its maw.
Across the slats of sun, across the street
My neighbor is at the end
Of his driveway picking up the daily newspaper.
He stands, notices me and waves.
I wave back with an easy smile.
Morning is broken neat and orderly
All the same.

Peugeot

I know the kid's an alcoholic
that he's into Peugeots, fixing
the machines given him by a
befriended Frenchman who is
a father-figure of sorts, helping
the kid moving forward in some
sort of style.
I know this kid's seen difficulties
dead end jobs, and aimlessness
because I know this to be true
I listen to his self-indulgent, auto-
graphical poetry with a smile.
I know all this because his daddy
already told me about his son
tore him down and threw up his hands
because of this I tell the kid he's
got real promise there in his words.
But I wished I'd told him, said to
him, hey, man one of these days
you're going love yourself, and
your daddy, well, he's going love
you too, enough to give you the
gift of promise for yourself, but mostly
give you the gift of pride.

Honey Made the Actor

1.

Honey made the actor
Richard Burton apoplectic
Even if he was in a room
With a jar
Its lid tight and in a drawer
It smothered some other
But what? — anxiety
Protects as salve some
Other deeper
Wound

2.

Martin says everything
We do is suffused with anxiety
Tying our shoelaces and dancing
Waiting for the train, running from the rain
Being in a room
With the hidden darkness of ourselves
Walking again in the light of day
All of it. Heidegger writes —
Pulling at the wires we keep
Alive in the furrows
Our antic heart

3.

— an interlude between reading —

Ancient rumor
About how we can't find our way
How all the gods
Have lost
Their way weed-strewn
Crazy blaring horns bent and trashed gutter
Bound, blinding petrol sun
We've all covered our eyes
Against what gathers
The throat, the taste of it
Still on the tongue
The cup of a man's heart
Runs over
Over with dateless expectancy

...But Dale
There's no yesterday or tomorrow
Just the day, Carnegie writes
Light compartments
Hold out your hand
Look
Them in the eye
Smile
Influence
Make friends

Asphyxia Benediction

Sylvia learned from Anne—Robert Lowell

Ubiquitous cigarette jutting obscure smoke
Curling umbrage through your Medusa-mad hair
Your jejune gaze taking in hegira's way
Recognizable then not
I call you Sexton to my Plath.
Me, looking at you, mystery of the opposite opposite sex—
That great bifurcation jigsaw puzzle piece—Lighter
As if rosary beads in stained hands.
How you've stripped your fingers of me tossing those strange bands of old
Left empty a doll's house for the garage to inhale cold exhaust
Escaping the way of sorrow, the way they lined us up
Boy girl boy girl boy girl
Boy, you're an arrow, you say, not the bow.
Still, I want to say we both have needs and quivers
Don't judge the succor by the shade of its skin.
Long ago we both gave up pink and blue for a stronger hue
of blood.
At some point, all that Sex-Ed is a slag
Heap of burnt ash now scorched by our fiery shibboleths
Flash points lost and meaningless. Sextants aimed
At vastly different bodies. Each of us a little adrift
Trail your hand in, you say, feel the nails
Build your own stasis don't borrow my words
What's bred in the bone births the riddle in your marrow.

Time was we played house and doctor
The Hardy Boys at your calling yet
Nancy Drew I never asked you to be my wife
Now we can't talk to each other? The crimes pile up,
The mansions remain haunted; clues are buried and forgotten.
Instead, you give the sign of choking yourself. You give
The asphyxia benediction—
Rats live on no evil star—figure it out back, straight.
Man, on my knees, recognizable, perhaps then not
Head inside a dark oven dying for a light
Shaking fingers forking up in front of your face in a V
Smoke concealing your secrets—
You are Sexton to my Plath.

Pocket Stars

We pocket our stars one constellation at a time
In our deepest moments, we alone reach the deep
Safekeeping guidance, its conceit twinkles brightly
Lighting our wanderlust way back home to the gazers…
Pointing there and there saying look they're dead.

Rabbit

In the tree-line shadow
A man wears a large hare's head
Naked from the waist down
Mud and blood splattered hopping.
Usually I would have
Kept going, instead I take one
Illegal highway switchback
Park by the side of the road.
Cutting through the grass quietly
At an angle to surprise the beast
Turns out to be a plastic shopping bag
Snared and screaming in the wind.
Riot of stripped limbs and quivering
Weeds, I fall into the waist-high wheatgrass
Crying. I've been so – tired
And looking back at my car
The terrible sight behind clutching the wheel.
A giant rabbit with a man's head turning, slowly
Chewing an enormous carrot, although
I couldn't
I couldn't be sure.

Rings

A golden ring arrives by post
To consider a new hand
Bestowed to my uncle in 1947
Matching the one given his brother
My father, when they reached 21
For years, I've worn my father's ring
Several times needing to be fixed
Its brother arrived from Down Under
In better shape, but close resemblance
Father died years ago. His brother just so
A few weeks into late summer, miles and miles away
Now a golden reunion whose reverberating
Rings will be found on other hands
One for my dear nephew a hulk of a man
The other to my own brother's son out west
Where this will end – I'm less certain
As we all are – rocks ripples ponds
Rings of gold are precious, but time still
The upper hand

Hurricane Rothko

(North apse triptych, Rothko Chapel, Mark Rothko)

Sibilant silence is accurate
As the chapel fills with rising octaves—

Hurricane Rothko nocturnal triptych opera
Nightfall voices widedeep wonder pockmark awe.
Thrum through, through furrows,
Bones, skin, teeth and vociferous mind
—Bible-black and vesper plum wine.
Revealing, heavy curtains bereft of stars,
Beauty whirling, weaving into patina skeins
Wrapping beholders of his darkest incantation.
Aware arising arias, voices in prayer—Preghiera,
Opens every opera, to passion, its pause
Every storm opens its rattle rage, its becalming eye.
Aftermath's wake leave mad gathering what may,
Rothko, shuddering, silence so finite, by his own
Deft hand, composing temporal sacred laments,
Slices his bothersome canvases, sighs razor's edge, and dies.
Blood burbling, falling
—Bible-black and vesper plum wine—
Splattering as absolute, God-given stars
Hangs himself high amongst the uprising voices.

—Voices, as if from the lungs of Simon whistling down Iscariot
Darkness smokes briefly alights as singed doves.

Black Wave

He keeps newspaper copy in his briefcase —
We are boats upon the open sea
Jostling through the jangle
— About the start of the war and its demands

What can be said of such things?
In waves, everything before him undulates
Behind dead yesterdays shatter into shrapnel
Dragging his body to work, over pit and metronome

He thinks —
Stars nothing but tossed
Universe empty, ebb swelling,
Enough to bring a man to his knees

There's always the gun to hold, to scream
Out a charge against the darkness
He opens his briefcase at the corner
Near his work pulling out

The obituary saying, he is dead
Flipside to the notice of war
Dullness awaits him like the bleeding
Through of one story to another

Ink stains on his fingers —
Though the names there are different
He knows all boats upon the sea
— Feels the coming wave

Awake

And out of bed
Chased by surly sea monsters riding Aegean pixels
Washed up here with a gloaming thick head
Of early morning's milky wading.

So far from home, it takes time to adjust
The light here viscous and foreign
Transfixed, transplanted and replaced
The lines of my life scribbled and rewritten.

Outside in this quiet and isolation
Standing on the edge of a driveway
Cat curling around my ankle, sanguine
Watching darkness broken by day.

Across the distance, Athena emerges
Part of a dark tree line, cupping
Her hands around her mouth instructing
Something, squinting helps to see.

I am Odysseus still far from home
Sailor tossed at sea by its angry master
She mouths *I love you*
Or, maybe it's *wake the fuck up.*

Blood & Phlegm

Cobalt churning sea waves capped white dirty
Still surfers cling to boards riding, swimmers diving
Under tattooed seawall and dungy dunes behind them
Me standing there defiant, secure in my reading.
There are two ways to take it in
With ignorance tossing in vast brine
Knowing its dark secrets.
Or stand, dry and away. Out. Motionless.
When choosing this way or its alternative
Envy sinks surely.
Assigning ourselves to solitary superiority
Standing outside, seemingly controlling
Water's way, its ragged wheezing, its blood & phlegm.
Unable to let go into the deep of it—
Death and garbage; unexpected treasures—
Lungs full of sparks, fear, thrashing about
under someone's hand.
The color I see is not right—it is opaquely rendered
Remaining blind, unknowable. A mystery.
Or a memory, distant, of losing control...
The taste of blood & phlegm
Fear diving under.

Dust

He cleaned up in anticipation of her arrival. He made things look right. He dusted the tables, the lamps, the curtains and the shelving. He pulled out books and CDs and cleaned behind them. He sprayed cleanser on the TV screen and wiped it clean. Everywhere he looked, dust. In places, the dust, beggar's velvet she called it, was so thick he wrote in it. Then he destroyed the evidence. He did not want her to see that he had not cleaned his apartment, that he never cleaned his apartment. Dust was a dead giveaway. There was never any dust in the house when he was growing up. Every Sunday after church his mother cleaned the house from top to bottom. She would mumble prayers as she dusted and vacuumed. He often wondered why she had to clean the house every weekend. Everything had it place. Dust did not settle. It was unsightly to her. Anything unclean was unsightly to his mother. She could not look at a dead cat on the side of the road. *Bury it,* she said. Open caskets frightened her; she did not see her own mother for the very last time as she lay in the final box. His mother even dusted the day she got the news her lump was malignant. She said, we always tidy up. She had a full mastectomy. With time to spare, he sat on the balcony and lit up a smoke. She was not expected for another hour. Tired as he often was now in the late afternoons, he sat and watched the blue smoke make moats in the air—then disperse. He was calming down. He did not hear her come in the apartment. He did not notice her footfalls as she came up behind. He only caught the tail end of, *Memento, homo, quia pulvis es, et in pulverem reverteris.* He brushed ash off his chest, and rose slowly.

Sweetness

Her son is in the hospital fed medicine intravenously. He is a child, perhaps under five, suffering and could die. She talks about playing with her son, helping him down the cold, hospital hallway with Mr. Drippy—a transparent, umbilical cord connected to a tall uncle of glass and steel. That is what sustains him and that is what she calls it. When she is asked. It is other things. To talk about it, she wants to describe it in the poetry of other things. Her son becomes a sestina, artifice. To find her words, she goes to the library. She calls it Vermont. She says it is sapping. She recalls maple trees. It is sweet. Her son chokes on syrup in his sleep. She tells him to swallow, slowly; the sestina is incomplete.

Jazz Messengers

Free jazz in the freezing
Fall morning – interrupted
Blue jay shrieking through
A porcelain sky overhead:
My favorite season —
So many new beginnings
Endings too – improvised
Or otherwise free
Art Blakey, Jazz Messengers
And me,
Oh, and that *fucking*
Blue jay
Excited it seems, like a poet
Opening the day's mail

Crow's Stones

Reminder stones, pebbles actually
On morning's window pane, carried
In a crow's maw, concrete colored
Stones on the pathway, newspaper
Kept intact by weighing invisible rocks,
My hands, coarse, callused, covered
Dust from granite, mineral mist news
Print memory a small heart shaped stone
Deep in my pocket, along with a crow's
Beak, asphalt hued too, moist and with
Spit and reminders, of the craggy hills
Looming in the day, horizon filling
Endless, accompanied each at its base
A large boulder for the pushing forth
To crumble into stones, pebbles actually
For a morning window pane reminder
There're hovering shadows
Murder of circling crows
Stones in concrete beaks.

One in a million

There's no lightning in these parts
Throat-clearing thunder to be sure
Rolling through like an old train
But no streaks of brilliantly jagged light
We hunt blind the Spanish moss shadows
By surd, scythe and cicada song
Deep into night's worrisome kudzu
Seeking that dark ground where long ago
All the bolts were buried, map burned
Leaving us little but bedtime stories
About how we've never been struck
Nor won the lottery.

Sisyphean Stones

Bigger than Tartarus buildings
Beget by Atlas shrugging off
Conquered men casting last stones
Deadheading sprogs without mothers
Not well enough to raise a heavy rock
Monsters, We, Stentorian, scream, scurrying
Back into brittle velvet ossuaries
Erected for easy genuflection, worshipping
Buildings built over broken bodies
Banners proclaiming: All is for sale!
Even those Sisyphean stones.

Ice Story

Every other year, an envelope arrives in the mail. Inside there is a single note with no author named and no one addressed. The note reads: *Do you hear the ice cracking?*

They would gather at the bridge in the morning, before the sun rose. It would always be in deep fall, when the temperature is cold enough to freeze water, but the snow has not yet fallen. They would sit under the bridge and lace up with ice skates.

The ice on the lake at that time of year is thin, but pristine. The sound it makes when the steel blades slice into it is magical. There is little friction and skaters glide effortlessly, smoothly.

For days, they would watch the weather, read the thermometer, just to be sure. They would scan the sky, read the papers, and listen intently to the radio. They would finally agree on a day.

The skate was over a mile long from one bank to another. Starting off was crucial. For a moment, there in the dark, their breath hanging in the air in front of their faces, they would stand in silence.

Then, *Go!*

As soon as the skates hit the ice, the ice begins to crack. They must be fast and cannot hesitate. They pump their arms; their legs scissor back and forth quickly. Their lungs grow cold. They cannot stop. It is all ahead.

Mostly they skate hard and fast, without looking back and without speaking. They are all listening.

As the dawn begins to thaw into daylight, and the bank comes into view they begin to glide, turning to see what is coming for them. Only then with strides left in the annual race do they breathlessly ask: *Do you hear the ice cracking?*

People noticed a change in them. They were quietly confident. They kept to themselves. The three boys never told anyone about it. Years have gone by and they no longer live in the same small town with the lake that freezes over in the winter. But occasionally, an envelope comes in the mail one of them thinks to send. They open it slowly and withdraw the single note.

Their lungs grow cold, and they listen.

Love Supreme

Coltrane low, daylight dying and we are all up for speed. We have been sitting with nothing much to do, and trying to come up with reasons why Jesus wouldn't puke if he returned. Money makes the world, not manna. Phil came up with that one an hour ago reading a rather tattered copy of *Parabola* he pilfered from the library. Phil's dead. At least his parents told him he was, after he told them what he told them. He is into self-forgetting. Almost. Shelly's glasses are low on her nose, nodding to 'Trane, sipping her Red Bull and speaking Hammarskjold. *Let me finish what I have been permitted to begin.* She's nothing since she left her job for art. Down the road, we stare at Mark Rothko's work and hum in the chapel for the operatic deities he built here. Rothko wanted the experience of staring at his paintings to mimic a sense of awe astronomers have staring at the night sky.

At night, when I cannot sleep, I make crucifixes using nine-inch carpenter nails cut on a lathe. That is how I make my living now; Christ is a living. Hawk 'em on Montrose Avenue, mumbling Rosaries for my tricking past. We are no Bible-thumpers. We sign ourselves when no one is around. We are a subversive wing of Opus Dei. We know we are all walking contradictions, we all realize this is nothing. Nothing is what happens when you're busy making other plans. Nothing happens when you are permitted to begin. We have nothing, now, but this faith. These nine-inch nails. The paintings of a man who hanged himself because of the things he saw in blank spaces. The rock, the risen, the promise of love supreme.

Shock

In any direction, when there is no snow, the horizon where I'm from fills with undulating fields of flaxen wheat, sometimes blond shocks and often dirtied bales squared or rounded and tied with ochre twine; and there, too often miles of wild green-white grasses enchanted by a nearly inaudible music, the traces of which only discernible as wind. In these parts, one who has seen the wind need only turn and gesture towards the tossing wheatgrasses' testimony of what cannot be immediately witnessed. Out there a system of endurance, an invisible mechanism triggered to ensure another season's promise. Ambling into the engulfing body of scratchy grasses, the spindly stocks and darkened loam (depending on conditions) rises rich and earthy with each inhalation as some kind of ancient memory. Eroded furrows funnel the searcher unknowingly through the fulgent, and at times fusty labyrinth, until one can duck down and take to holding tiny wax plated leaves in their insignificant fingers, and marvel at how these tiny shields, tactile like corrugated cardboard, hold their moisture. When its drier, when there's drought, the simple wonder of how these leaves curl in on themselves, upward, to form a narrow tube to lessen its exposure to what it lacks. And knowing, but not understanding, how its stomata, like raised hands in exaltation, secure succor and survive. A fecund fortitude silently wired by mystical rhizomes reaching out beneath the weathered ground brings one to a mesmerizing halt. Being amongst this splendor and envisioning the endless seasons passing, is to understand the slow accretion of that green fuse the poets are wont to pitch rhapsodically, and how this same force, quietly, incessantly, over and through the majesty of our own making sings in our blood — no less a shock at how utterly sublime our dance is to music nearly indiscernible save our entranced swaying. *Sub rosa,* one might say in resurfacing, rising and wading back through the amber unfolding.

Work

There is no poetry
In Fall yard work
Raking up the dead
Leaves, bagging it up
For the curb, to over-seed
Fertilize and spread that
Fecund earthy peat moss
It's back-breaking, oxygen-
Depriving, exhausting work you
Don't even see until another
Season rolls along to worry
Your labor —
Oh.
Oh, wait, dear reader
You got there before me
Of course; of course
My tiredness brings me
This thought:
Anything of worth
Takes great effort
Yard work poetry
Both, reap what
You sow

Wm. Anthony Connolly is the author of three novels *The Jenny Muck, Get Back* and *The Obituaries*, which was a Canadian bestseller. His work has appeared in *The Rumpus, Intellectual Refuge* and *Elephant Journal* to name a few. This is his debut poetry collection. He is on the faculty of the MFA in Writing at Lindenwood University, St. Charles, Missouri, and has taught academic writing in Texas and Kansas. A first-generation university student, he has earned a PhD in English and Creative Writing from the University of Missouri, and an MFA in Writing from Goddard College in Plainfield, Vermont. He and his wife Dyan and their two dogs, Hemingway Short Story and Professor Leo Tolstoy, currently reside in the Lone Star State.

www.ingramcontent.com/pod-product-compliance
Lightning Source LLC
Chambersburg PA
CBHW020123130526
44591CB00032B/492
* 9 7 8 1 9 5 0 3 8 0 1 9 0 *